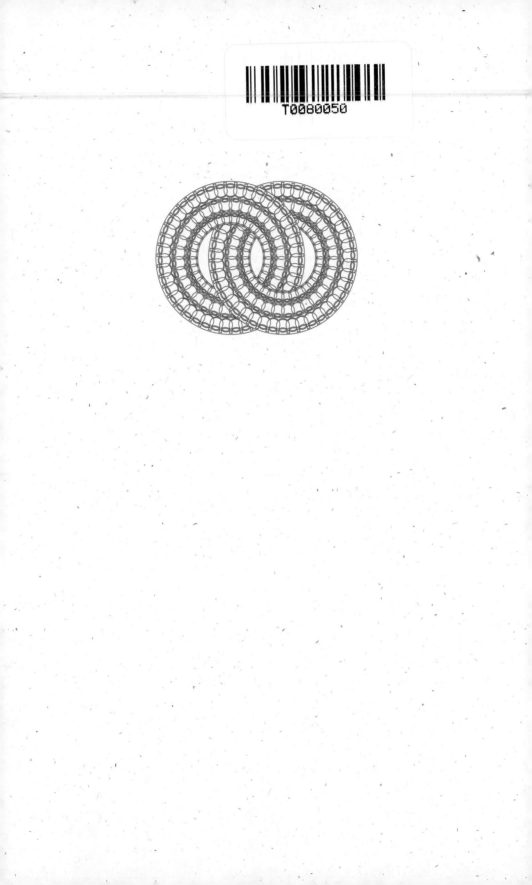

CRACKED PIANO

CRACKED

PIANO

MARGO

TAFT

STEVER

CAVANKERRY
PRESS

CavanKerry Press Ltd.
Fort Lee, New Jersey
www.cavankerrypress.org

Publisher's Cataloging-In-Publication Data
(Prepared by The Donohue Group, Inc.)
Names: Stever, Margo Taft, author.
Title: Cracked piano / Margo Taft Stever.
Other Titles: Laurel books.
Description: First edition. | Fort Lee, New Jersey : CavanKerry Press, 2019.
Identifiers: ISBN 9781933880709
Subjects: LCSH: Reason—Poetry. | Subconsciousness—Poetry. | Thought and
    thinking—Poetry. | Loneliness—Poetry.
Classification: LCC PS3569.T4573 C73 2019 | DDC 811/.54—dc23

Book design and typesetting by Mayfly Design
First Edition 2019, Printed in the United States of America

Cracked Piano is the 14th title of CavanKerry's Literature of Illness imprint. LaurelBooks are fine collections of poetry and prose that explore the many poignant issues associated with confronting serious physical and/or psychological illness.

CavanKerry Press is grateful for the support it receives from the New Jersey State Council on the Arts.

for Donald Stever

Contents

/ *FOUR*

/ *FIVE*

Introduction

Margo Taft Stever's searing poems in *Cracked Piano* evoke the sense of desolate aloneness that was experienced by her great-grandfather, Peter R. Taft, when he was institutionalized as a young man at the Cincinnati Sanitarium. As was the custom in the 1870s and later, Peter was put away in an asylum when he acted strangely. With no detailed accounts of his symptoms, it is impossible to make a diagnosis from our vantage point many years later. However, there are some clues that he did not have a major mental disorder.

Prior to his hospitalization, Peter was known as a brilliant man, first in his class at Yale. But when he contracted typhoid fever and was treated with calomel, a compound laced with mercury, he developed terrible headaches—a side effect of mercury poisoning. We don't know if he had other mercury-associated mental symptoms such as lethargy, memory impairment, or hallucinations. However, we do know from his letters (appearing as found poems in this book) from the asylum that he wrote in a clear, well-organized manner with none of the confusion or psychosis of ongoing mercury poisoning or of significant mental illness. Instead, there are aching pleas to be reconnected with his family and the world. One wonders if Peter was shut away because of a mistaken diagnosis and erroneous theories of the medical profession at the time coupled with embarrassment of his socially prominent family. His half-brother, William Howard Taft, went on to become the president of the United States in 1909.

Peter's physician at the Cincinnati asylum, Dr. W. S. Chipley, the superintendent, had no specialty training in psychiatry and, from entries in medical journals, appears to have been primarily interested in the maintenance of hospital buildings and the cost of care. Chipley wrote letters to Peter's family giving advice that is the polar opposite of treatment methods used today. In essence, he prescribed almost complete isolation from his loved ones.

Peter speaks of his abject disconnection in the poem, "Cracked Piano," for which the book is named: "I am alone this evening as every, / alone." His poignant yearning is captured in a found poem, a letter to his father, when he pleads for a visit from his wife who has been told to stay away: ". . . it will do me more good than anything that could happen." Peter asks his father to give "a kiss to the baby" because he can't touch the child. In today's psychiatric treatment, hospital stays are very short, family contact is encouraged, and specific therapies such as family therapy and cognitive-behavior therapy have been shown to have strong positive effects on treatment outcome. Sadly, Peter did not have this type of psychiatric care. We know little about his life after he left the asylum, but he died at forty-four of tuberculosis—a condition that he might have contracted there.

Among the wealth of poems with great emotional intensity in this volume, "The Lunatic Ball" is my personal favorite. I thought of Peter, a man with huge promise who now found himself a specimen behind glass, almost like a caged animal in a zoo, as the rich and privileged took their entertainment watching the "madmen" dance. Stever writes: "Behind a glass wall, well-dressed spectators, riveted, / sit amused. Looking at them looking, the patients // know they are through."

The poems in *Cracked Piano* take us to dark and painful places. To me they ask, is there a way out from these places? Is there hope for those who "know they are through"? We can learn from Peter and the others Margo Taft Stever brings to life in her poems and do our best to steer a different path.

—Jesse H. Wright, M.D., Ph.D.

\ \ \ / \ \ \ / \ ONE \ /

Idiot's Guide to Counting

How do you become one
with the horse, riding and becoming
the act of riding,
and the horse becoming the self
and the other at exactly
the same second, counting strides,
counting muscle movement,
counting fences, hurtling over
them with the horse, counting
the everything
of one?

How do you count, how do you
pull a muscle turning over
in bed at night—measurements
that change everything, counting
back to everything, the everything
of one, the pulled muscles of the back
of one, the entanglement
of one, the waves of particles
counting back, the quantum?

How to become one with
the branches of a tree, a grandfather
tree in an apple orchard
that no longer exists?
Separate one
from tree, horse,
counting numbers, counting
the grandfather tree
to find the solution of
one.

Counting trees, leaves, counting
everything as no longer
existing, counting
trees as one with the everything
that no longer exists.

The Worst Mother

Playing music
for you before
you were born,
waking up so early,
we searched
the neighbor's yard
for sticks and pebbles.

We fed your puppy,
lizards, gerbils,
the mouse-eating
toad from Nepal.

The night you gagged
and choked up shreds,
as if your very insides
came out, as if
you could not stop
unloading
yourself of yourself,
I comforted you.

But you have forgotten
and you accuse,
as you remember
the deprivations—
that I cannot cook,
that I never fed you.

Now you profess
to care about nothing.
Someday you will forget
all of this, too—
the arbor, the green vale,
rushing out

toward the rushing creek,
the monitored hallway,
the anxious greeting.

See, instead, this picture
of you as a child
with bare feet—
the one in which you wore
cherub's wings,
gossamer everywhere.

Glimpse of an Infant Eating

Cupid never had wings.
Like you
      he gummed
          the apple
down
          to the core;

he, too, wanted to eat
the pit,
     the stem,
         the entirety.

Stepmother

Pricked by the yellow pinpoints of stars,
her wolf children howl in the night.
Homeless, following crumbs, they burrow
into caves of dying bats, barely warm.
Pine needles draw their blood.

A stepmother is always bitter,
rash, always seizing the rice,
the beans, the family
fodder. Don't step on a crack—step
on a stepmother, break her back.

The stepmother's fangs lengthen
in moonlight. Eating toads, she lives
in a mushroom forest. A poison comb
under her black cape taints apples for orphan
girls, seven feral children, all language forgotten.

A stepmother is always evil,
marked by the blood of her husband's children.
She tries to climb into the others' shoes.
Wrench, crack, break her back—step
on a stepmother, step on a stepmother.

Wind Innuendo

So small
she cannot talk,
the child sits
in a field of
daffodils.
Her face
held close
to the blossoms
turns
slightly yellow
in sunlight.

Pollen grinds into
her hands.
Stems tickle her
backbone, thread
into her skin.

The thick
strings of stamen
lick her tongue.
Her petals bend,
always in wind.
To insects that enter,

each movement is
innuendo.
Her body opens
and opens, swills
in the billowing
spring light.

Foghorn

Biddeford Pool, Maine

Mother, mother blistered down,
your dreams have drunk too much.

Band-aids rip your skin; blue-
black bruises mottle your arms.

Drinking sleep into your body
like a starvling come to food,

as if you never could sleep
enough, the long-winded ashes

of sleep, damp with verbena
sleep, the spectral vocabulary,

the torn covers of sleep; you
erase yourself from bed.

Whether you will rise up to yell
for your dead husband or crack

a plate on your grandson's
head. Whether you will wander

the streets in your nightgown
or bang pots in the kitchen.

No one can live on Wood Island,
across the channel from the summer

house where the first of your three
husbands died too young; the fog

horn is too deafening. Seagulls and
cormorants raise chicks in tumult.

The blurt
of the foghorn gone amok,

a foghorn that won't give up,
sometimes no matter how

clear or cloudless, an awful
insistence.

My Mother Is Dying

In the place where she belongs,
suffering erases itself, doves
bring her seeds, horses sleep
next to her in the straw,

> where she belongs; a welcoming
> place holds her, keeps her
> from running away—the green
> greenness of the hay turning to gold.

Already, the rain's restless
trajectory. My mother is busy dying;
she no longer knows my name.
This is the wind of Eden,

> the wand of change, the last slave
> of silence, the knave of rain, so quiet
> the roving of each vacant quest. Let her
> be buried in the sea by the seaberry,

the briar rock, the fossil chamber.
Alone, blown, roadside stray,
the flown restless wayward ringing,
bells clang, ocean downcast, rolls.

> Wandering once again, now I
> return to the center, searching
> the level earth, calling her name,
> remembering that I am lost.

The path unfurls before my dog
and me, walking to the rocks, the ocean
on one side, the bay on the other,
eiders blessing the waves.

The seagulls' spontaneous burst,
how it hurts with the radio blaring.
My mother is dying, gone from
a body that has abandoned her.

Cry because everything goes haywire,
because this is Apollo's siren lyre, the field-worn
answer, the childless response, children waiting
for some god to bring them home.

\ \ \ / \ \ / \ TWO \ /

The Lunatic Ball

after Dance in a Madhouse,
by George Bellows, 1882–1925

Furious dancing gives way to screams;
five men stare, ghoulish, at the wall.
This is the lunatic ball.

The best student Yale had ever seen:
three months after graduation, typhoid—
brain swelled inside his skull.

They dosed out calomel—five ghosts appeared
in a mercury dream, headaches unbearable.
This is the lunatic ball.

Married one year, baby the next, his wife
filed for release; the medical textbooks
he gleaned: futile, endless stall.

A woman names her baby doll Christ, lurches,
leans, a building in an earthquake, then
she crawls. This is the lunatic ball.

One man plays a flute, calls himself Faunus;
another uses an invisible latrine.

Attendants haul out a wildman in a straitjacket
on a wooden beam; a woman growls like a bear.
This is the lunatic ball.

Behind a glass wall, well-dressed spectators, riveted,
sit amused. Looking at them looking, the patients

know they are through. Spectacled
men sport greatcoats, and laced-up
women make jokes in the shimmering hall.

Something Wrong

Cincinnati Sanitarium
Private Hospital for the Insane
College Hill, Ohio
March 27, 1878

Mrs. P. R. Taft,

Your note is received
and the trunk for Peter.

I am pleased to have to say
that he is getting along
much better than I suspected,
in quiet, and takes
outdoor exercise. The best
indication is that he is
becoming conscious
of his condition.
He said that he was not aware
that his health was impaired,
either mental or physical,
but he now perceives
that there must have been
something wrong.
I will let you know if his
comfort or welfare
requires anything more.

Respectfully,
    W. S. Chipley, M.D.

Cracked Piano

Cincinnati Sanitarium
Private Hospital for the Insane
April 2, 1878

Dear Father,

I am alone this evening as every,
alone. An artist of imperfect
mind is endeavoring to extract
harmonious discords out of a cracked
piano just at my left. Life here
is of the plainest, I might say,
of the hardest kind.

Last Sunday, Mr. and Mrs. John
Whetstone came to this institution
to see her brother, but Mrs. W. spent
some time on this floor. She stayed
all night of Sunday and until noon
Monday. Her visit was a godsend to me.

Tell Tillie that I have enjoyed
the fruit and preserves. Tell Tillie
that it hurts me to write her, but if
she will come and see me, it will do me
more good than anything that could
happen. My foot is sore and needs
a healing application.

Each patient has a separate room
with a carpet, a bed, a table,
a washstand, a box, and one chair,
but no gas and no candles.
There are two tables, one for

the sane portion of this community—
one table for the patients, the other

for the attendants. At the head
of the patients' table sits Colonel Passot
who is never guilty of two consecutive
ideas. He is, moreover, quite dirty.
On his right side sits your son.
On Colonel Passot's left resides
a Mr. Williams who cannot articulate

so as to make himself understood.
He consists principally of hair.
Next to him sits his special attendant,
Mr. O'Brien, and on the right
side of your son rests a small German,
the Duke, with whiskers and eyeglasses.
He is constantly saying things

that strike him as witty, and he laughs.
He is a good deal of a fool.
On the table further down
sits Mr. McNeal, the tormentor
of the piano, and a Mr. Gillespie
who has been here for about a year.
He is going away in May.

The latter has privileges
to go out without attendant.
Further on is a thick-faced
individual who never speaks,
and whom I will denominate
as Mr. Blank.

The conversation is neither amusing
nor instructive. It is liberally
interspersed with grunts by Mr. Williams,

the man of hair, or hearty laughs
by the young man from Illinois.
But the bottom of the page is reached.

A kiss to the baby.

Your affectionate son,
    Peter

Plank Walk

Cincinnati Sanitarium
Private Hospital for the Insane
April 7, 1878

Dear Father,

Sunday has come again and gone. The doctor allowed me
to move into the cottage. It is retired and quiet, has none
of the unpleasant associations connected with the upper story.

At our table are Mr. Sheets, the steward, and his wife; Dr. Savage,
the assistant physician; a Judge Johnson, who is staying here, hailing
from the South; and your son. No one knows why Judge Johnson
is staying here. I have tried to find out in what particular part of his mental
or physical structure the deficit exists that requires his confinement
in this solitude, but the only item of intelligence elicited is that
he has been cross at home, that he is staying here because
his family wants to keep him here.

The plank walk that you and I would answer for the purpose
of exercise does not seem to meet the case. I never tried walking
on a plank walk before. But it is the hardest thing to walk on that I ever
got hold of. It is not possible for the foot of mortal man to stand
walking on it for any considerable length of time. I have been on it for
half a day, and my feet are so sore and bruised that I had to come in
long before I wanted to, because my feet would not stand further service
in that way. It is a perfect means of torture to move for any length
of time upon that walk.

> Love to you all,
> Your loving and obedient son,
> *Peter*

P.S. Will you please tell Tillie that I want a pair of thin-soled gaiters?
I think there is a pair at No. 592 Freeman Street. If not, A. Hirsch
on Walnut Street under the Gibson House has my measurements
and can make a pair to suit. The shoes that I am wearing hurt my feet.

Causes of Mortification

Cincinnati Sanitarium
Private Hospital for the Insane
College Hill, Ohio
May 22, 1878

Dear Sir,

I was feeling satisfied with the progress
your son was making. It cannot be but
slow and gradual, but I cannot answer
for the consequences if he has many such

visitors as the gentleman who came
with your card. Your son requires, above
all things, quiet, and is in no condition
to be talked to about travel or a return

to housekeeping, or to be dosed with
ginger pop. These things gave him a bad
night, and he is not as well today. He is
the subject of disease that requires

medication and no amount of reason
can have other than a prejudicial effect.
The less said to him of himself and his
relations to others, the better.

If the Brain is restored to its normal
condition, all of his relations to others
will appear in the proper light. It is
desirable for one in his condition

to abstract the mind as much as
possible from self and engagement
from other matters. His attitude toward
his wife and the injurious effects

of her attention to him are not just
causes of mortification. These things
are common to almost all cases
of insanity; indeed, a notable disturbance

of the affective functions rarely fails
to be a marked characteristic of the malady.
Hence very few persons recover in the midst
of home surroundings and in association

with those who, in health, they most
devotedly love. I will be pleased to have
an interview with his stepmother if she
so desires it. I will make it convenient to call

almost any afternoon that may suit her.

Yours truly,
  W. S. Chipley, M.D.
  Superintendent
  Private Hospital for the Insane

No Occurrence of an Exciting Nature

College Hill
May 23, 1878

Dear Father,

The time is rolling along here slowly.
I seat myself in the office that is
pretty well filled with people playing
cards, writing, and talking. Letters
have not been very abundant here
this week, from home.

I wrote to Annie on Tuesday, and want
you to read the letter as it was intended
equally for you. No occurrence of an
exciting nature has transpired since
the dance of last Saturday night.

Tonight there is an arrangement for a
play in the hall. I saw by the paper
that you presided recently at an
oratorical tournament at St. Louis.
Everything is very quiet in this

vicinity. There have been no new
accidents in the narrow gauge, so
far as heard from. Night before last
we had an exciting game of Boston.
The chips are denominated dollars

instead of the numbers, and thus a
financial appearance is given to the
transaction. At the last game there
were as high as 1500 dollars in the
box and great excitement.

The winner has been trying to collect
ever since. It is a pretty hard crowd
to collect from, and a collection
taken up would probably not have
exceeded fifty cents. As a financial

center, this institution is not a success.
The wealthiest of the patients
are generally the old soakers who
came here to straighten up. But
their pile rarely exceeds a dollar,

and before long is considerably
impaired. I sent you by Mrs. Whetstone
some time since that I wanted the old
hunting case watch that I got when
in Paris. Mrs. Whetstone and her

husband were out last evening,
and took supper with the Doctor.
But I am tired this morning
and will have to close here.

Your affectionate son,
    Peter

Dr. Chipley is in the city today.

Common Cases of Insanity

Cincinnati Sanitarium
Private Hospital for the Insane
College Hill, Ohio
June 15, 1878

You do not seem to have received
my last note in which I gave you
your son's notion of the effect
of the visits and letters of his friends.
It is neither surprising nor a bad omen

that he is disinclined to the attentions
of his best friends. I was rather
surprised that at first, he seemed
pleased with such attentions, as
the reverse is the rule in almost

all such cases. I do not observe
any marked change in his condition.
His physical improvement is obvious
enough and mentally he seems
to be making such progress

as is common in such cases, but this
is always so gradual in cases like his,
as not to be notable from day to day.
So far, I see nothing peculiar
or remarkable in his case and think

there is naught to do but to persevere
in the course of treatment that
obviously lends to success.

Yours truly,
    W. S. Chipley
    Superintendent
    Private Hospital for the Insane

\ \ \ / \ \ \ / \ THREE \ /

I have been my arm

resting on the side of a truck,
carrying a cigarette
to my mouth—
my hand, an animal
that cannot see or hear.

Hudson Line

The river stretches out
like a line of flight, a pattern
winging toward God.
The river sucks
oars down; it pulls
toward depth, toward
study of the under-soul.
The river is constant.

The frozen forgotten earth
no longer speaks a language.
The dogs bark next door
at the clicking heels of the woman
who makes her way to the station.

Passengers stare at me on the train
at Spuyten Duyvil—their metallic drift
of perfumes, their attempts
to read as I write this line.

The river just stretches
with the Tappan Zee Bridge
into the green haze. No river
can deny the existence
of God, nor can trains travel
backward with people
shouting blindly out of windows.
This is a little train of reason.

People cough on trains;
something sticks like silkworms
to the backs of their throats,
and we who do not yet have coughs
have no time for mercy.

This is a train of thieves, all of us
who never cared for our jobs or our mothers,
who looked out on the Hudson
and saw only water.

Missing Link

This is an ancient lake,
swallowed by dreams
of unborn babies,
fossil fuel for fires,
unending, excrement
marked with bones
of mice and shrews.

Sediment is
thick and layered.
Each child is mine,
each special
smile, each toothy grin,
such pain
around the edges.

I hug the infants close
to shelter them from dogs.
Hyenas digest bones.
Nothing holds
together anymore.
Blankets flap apart.
The babies' legs are cold and kick;

the dogs are moving in.

Valentine

The night dragons first banged
at the door, their iron claws sparked
on the brass knocker, black masks

sewn right into their skin.
Dragons crept back again last
night, fire-breathing, restless

turning of their bodies, searching
for stones, for powder, anything
to keep back the dust. Dragons

prefer pitch darkness, the kind
that shows nothing and children
fear most, where anything grows

quickly—spores, mushrooms, ticks.
Sleep marchers rode into me,
and I could not move or dream.

I became a vast and starless chasm,
the lights long since surrendered
and the rushing wind bound

the swamp grass down.
The wings of twilight moths
against the screen—something

about the pillow held your scent. I think
of what I would do without you.

Drought

A dry spell
wavers on the page;
heat burns off words.
Useless articles
pile up like trash.
I plow them into hills.
Small silences, words like
"it" and "but," clatter together
in memory of what's
unexpressed. Reassembled,
they could be bones, meadows,
offerings to the gods.

Here is a mound of bones,
woman with infant.
Her breasts are wilted.
Below bellowing surfaces
that cry out for food,
angular bones
pierce through paper-thin flesh.

The verbs linger longest,
out of alignment, months later,
hardest to forget. They knock together,
lonely for ancient villages,
the specificity of snow.
A thousand times each day
I think of death, the villages of
people on their knees, sowing
children into rows like seeds.

The mother and child starve.
Leaves on the trees blur
behind their backs.
I stare out of windows
for signs of passing shadows,
but the neighborhood looks the same,
houses set on foundations,
people posing mutely behind closed doors.
The rancid glow of streetlights
colors the road with hollowness,
the line in the middle
almost lost in the glare.

Invisible Fence

So many people have moved in.
I don't know them anymore.
I don't know their names.
Not even my dreams make sense.

The birds have flown up from the privet.
They don't know that the door
jams aren't square, that something
is very wrong in this house.

All my friends have left for the country,
and I alone stand on the sidewalk,
staring into closed suburban windows,
fixating on muffled arguments.

Even my own dog won't stay. The invisible
fence advisers leave cryptic messages
on my answering machine about restraining him.
They are baffled by his

arrogance, his willingness
to approach the electric wire,
as if nothing at all could shock him.
Someone I have never met

climbs secretly up a ladder
onto the porch of our new addition.
He is purple, a statue
in the most conceptual museum.

Cold water drips from the sink.
Drip rhythm: Two drips.
Two drips. Two drips.
Only the cold water drips.

Voices bubble up in the neighborhood,
human sounds mixed with the bark of dogs,
gas flames of cookouts.
Sometimes I think about nothing

except a few birds and the rain—how they
continue to sing even when it's raining,
even when the cold raining rain
refuses to stop.

Surfaces

Take possession
of the blanket, the feel
of it, the smooth

and the lean, the lying
down of it, the way it
imitates the body.

This is the promise
I keep—to rest on the
bed under moonlight.

Yet so many cats
knead the surfaces;
their paws tap-dance,

wishing for food.
The dark summer
storm rips across

the bed, rumpling
covers like waves,
whitecaps against

each other.
Cats' paws skim
the sheets as if

called by a higher spirit.
Their willowy bodies
curl together in sleep.

Beulah Reid

The switches line up
by your bed, wolves' teeth,
and you, cruel nanny,
use them in your finest dreams.
Your nose mounts a grand plot
to take over your face
each time you show us
the noise birches make.
The sticks we find outside,
you turn against us.
Some are blunt, others sharp,
spring-loaded. You twist them before us.

Rustling and rumbling
through underbrush with packs
of dogs, we smell of rotting
leaves, everything going back, the rough
welter blending into earth.
One night you crack the window.
You hiss with damnation
even a preacher couldn't better—
"You kids ain't nothin' but a bunch of hillbillies."

Night after night I witness
your red vinyl rocking chair,
your stockings pulled down over ankles,
the corridors of your white bulging
legs, your jutting veins, while bubbles
float over *The Lawrence Welk Show*,
and Liberace pounds his piano
with dumb passion.

Hand

Cell and bone
more servile than the elbow
and more birdlike

than the nose.
Thin fingers fan out
like spokes on a half-moon

wheel, or the toes of a balled
Chippendale claw.
A hand can be a monastery,

fingers bent in repose,
or a slaughterhouse
where nothing is safe.

The True Story of Eugene

I.

Two brothers discovered him
beside the road somewhere in the thickening
underbrush between Columbus and Cincinnati.
He was dead, black, nameless, without clothes,
perfect for their display.

They embalmed him, laid him out
under chicken wire, called him Eugene.
People flocked past his splintered bier,
gawked at the marvel of a man
so unidentified, so perfectly preserved.

II.

"Onion, octopus, 3, 2, 1,
kiss the girls and make them run."
He tore off the clothes in his dream
and fell against thorns.
He saw a man with a flashlight
who first called all the fireflies
to him, then lit up a cave.
Worms dangling from the walls
dug into his body.

So much of what was inside
him was stripped bare.
He could shelter nothing beneath his limbs.
He stayed where he was beside the road.

III.

We were children then and stopped
to visit the ramshackle shed
where Eugene lay in state.

His body looked unbuttoned, flap
by flap. Straw knocked against straw,
the hush of sleeves.

Outside, a wasp nest fell on the sidewalk,
all the autumn wasps dead.
It looked like something decapitated,
like so many burnt-out cigars stuck together.

Why So Many Poets Come from Ohio

Some say El Niño blows them
over the Rockies, and poets pool
like guppies grounded
by the plains, hollowed into Ohio.

How easy it is to forget the nameless
places along the scant
unremarkable rivers, the burning
polluted creeks. Even horses

pull themselves back from the earth
to ignore where they were born.
Why poets come from Ohio explains
why shopping malls are built to last

only decades, why deer end up dead on I-80.
Poets come from Ohio because
of the homelessness of the hills,
how they are low and huddled,

as if long ago glaciers ran out of energy
on the alluvial plain, leaving them
unstated, looking westward for relief.
Poets who wish to intone

come from Ohio because nothing happens,
only the sonorous gestation of their interiors.
They search the soured hills for daffodils, for turnips,
for everything they thought once grew there.

Perimeter

Another apocalypse. Spit out
what is possible. Glass surrounds you,

imploded glass of houses,
bones, books, breasts, teeth, cars.
Not one of these is replaceable,

even if glass returns to sand.
On the black, volcanic beach

bodies press against you,
rooting out the value of sand.
The sun goes into you,

an empty closet. Doors
shut around the perimeter.

This bed of glass brings
viscous blood to the surface.
Here the torsos of dolls

lie faceless, embedded after war
to prove things endure.

Queen City

Coming back to Cincinnati,
a wayward soul looking for a sign, I see the city
stretching out like a foresworn promise.

The thing next to cleanliness—Cincinnati—
host to Proctor & Gamble, the Smut Buster,
Skyline Chili. I now return like a blind man

inhabiting a woman's body, an alien
within an alien, hopelessly lost, sensing Cincinnati
will always be foreign. The city will always catapult me

to a childhood endlessly spinning
out of control. Cincinnati, oh city of fountains,
squares, new buildings I will never recognize,

what is your plan? Returning to the once great
Queen City, riverboat town, gateway to the south, I find
ghosts of the underground railroad, Mapplethorpe, race

riots, boycotts. Cincinnati, where crows combed the outlying
fields in awful stillness, and dogs barked as if they alone
knew their voices echoed for miles down hollows,

where are you now? Where is the Cincinnati filled
with concrete strength, suppressed love, waiting breath,
this city of my youth with everything opening, where smells

of spring meant daffodils covered whole hillsides
with yellow? City once called Porkopolis, where hordes of pigs
pushed pedestrians off streets, once trashed

by Frances Trollope, why am I coming back to you, land
restlessly stolen, abandoned in adolescent
despair, vanished island, lost promise of light?

Quiet, with Trees

> the distress of the song
> cuts through an ample silence
> —*William Carlos Williams*

Sit on any porch
with your infant
in quiet
with the trees,
curious of their
forbearance
in the traffic.

A truck appears, and
a man lumbers out.
"Are you the lady
who called about
a branch
on an electric wire?"

Tell him that you called
a week ago, and men
came at 3:00 a.m.
to cut the limb down.

Watch him climb into
his cherry picker anyway.
Tarzan, he darts upward
through the ample trees.
The child clings to you
as branches crash
onto the sidewalk.

Strange Familiarities of Death

The man who had no hope
of dry cleaning burnt his store
to get insurance. The army
chaplain spoke of a mushroom
cloud as beautiful. Generals

shredded reports of danger.
"This bomb is only a test,"
the radio blurted. The women
of St. John, Utah, saw
the cloud rise, the searing wind.

Soldiers lowered into foxholes.
"You have nothing to fear.
Stay inside your houses."
The force of the wind was
molten iron blowing over them.

Blood ran from their eyes.
They could see bones
through their skin. The earth
burned their feet. The snow
when it came later was gray.

Van Gogh to His Mistress

He sensed his ear,
but he could
not see it.
In the blind
this is called
blindsight.

The last failed
effort
of the body
to survive—
*Keep this
object carefully.*

The ear rested
on the table
alone
among blue tints
and suppressed
shadows.

To present
an ear
in the middle
of the night,
an arterial flap,
flap of
bat's wing,
wing of angel.

Yellow Raincoat

Why did you
swim out
on the ocean,
unprovoked,
wearing only
a yellow raincoat?

When we race
to the beach
and find
your stranded shoes
on the narrow
spit of sand,
we know
you are out there
daring us
to save you.

Your eyes
and their absences
stick to us
like tentacles
and draw us
to the waves.

They back us
into sand dunes
with our ropes
and life vest, dreading
the competence
of our instruments.

Receiving the Ashes

I.

She forgot to ask him something.
She forgot what she forgot to ask.
The TV evangelists committing
adultery made the news.

She would never be famous.
She could not imagine sex
with a TV evangelist—
how some women would do
anything to be saved.

II.

She stood on the sidewalk.
Her small boy looked down,
plumbed the depths of the storm sewer.
She looked away for a moment,
and when she looked back,
she could hear him far below.
His voice was a breaking thread.
She had nothing to hold onto.

III.

Some doctors say ridges
on ears predict heart failure,
and the whorls of fingerprints
circumscribe our lives
like the skin of a cucumber.

IV.

The UPS man delivers her ashes
in a cardboard box.

Among the boxes
in her brother's garage
this is the smallest.

Condor, hawk, shrike,
how many birds can fill the night;
how many birds are sleeping?
How many birds hunt—their claws
glint, chance the moonlight?

Nothing's Holding Up Nothing

El Salvador, 1982

Under the floorboards with the wood
rot, the insects, ants skittering to
and fro, the mother hides with her child.
Her nipple's in the infant's mouth,
but her milk won't let down.

She did nothing, but the officials
suspected, decided to make an example,
the child dragged out, beaten,
the bellies of flowers, blackened,
the bells, the bells,
the long toll of roots . . .

It is hard to believe anything
was ever alive under here, under
these boards, anything alive
for long under these boards.
Filaments break off and powder
as if they never were wood,
as if the hollows were roads
going somewhere, as if the mother's
breasts could fill with milk, as if
her child could breathe again.

Splitting Wood

It was the thought of his entering
their infant's room that drove her.

She remembered his face the first time
she saw him. Now, half gone from whiskey,
eyes hooded like a hawk's,
he said he'd kill the children when he woke.

The neighbors heard it,
the screams. They heard.

His workman's hand,
his gnarled hand dangled down.
The knife lay by the bed.
She slipped from the covers
while he slept, placed her feet
on the floorboards just so.

The dogs barked outside, snapdragons,
flowered tongues, and all the wired
faces of the past strung up. The ax
hung on the porch, woodpile nearby,
each log plotted, uneasily entwined.
The children's tears were rain,
tears were watering the parched hills.

The wild moon foamed at the mouth.
The wild moon crept softly at her feet.

The arms that grabbed the ax
were not her own,
that hugged it to her heart
while he slept were not hers,
the cold blade sinking in his skin.
She grew up in the country splitting wood.
She knew just how much it took
to bring a limb down.

Horse Fair

after The Horse Fair,
by Rosa Bonheur, 1822–1899

In men's clothes,
she makes herself
invisible to examine
anatomy at
the slaughterhouse.
She obtains
a police permit
to wear trousers
while she sketches.

At the horse fair,
she draws horses
pulling, snorting,
heads bumping,
thrashing, hooves
pounding, tails wringing,
charging forward,
rearing, bucking, wheeling,
disappearing into darkness.

Hooves hammer, whips
crack, horses writhe
between seer and seen,
the fairground a battleground.
Frenzied pitch, cymbals
clash, arms flail, whips
raised against the horses' arched
and shining necks.
Eyes bulge, terrified—
the dappled gray, the roan pull
away, toward thunder.

Raven's Rock

Sleepy Hollow, New York

Ichabod, the Headless
Horseman, rolling hills, the Highlands,
villages where men tarry at the bars,
sleepy towns—Beekmantown, Tarrytown,
but who has heard of three young women
who lost their way in separate incidents
many years apart, who took shelter
at Raven's Rock and perished in the night?
Who knows why they walked the tree-
frozen road, their fingers burnt with cold?

Three figures in white—their ethereal,
shrill pitch unbearable,
gesturing, as if the swirling snow,
eddies of snow, snow rivers
could be human, as if something
totally frozen could be alive.

What is a raven but a bird, a ghost
but a raven bird, and the ghosts of three women
ravenous, waiting at Raven's Rock
for a single man to pass by,
and did they vent their rage
for ages of wrongness,
for the unrequited, the undone love,
love forced upon them, jealous love
hardening them, these women
by the Hudson now still,
now irrevocably gone.

Virgin Cult

Outside peasant women shrouded with
winnowing sheets plow fields; their mitts
clot with dirt, feet rag-wrapped in mud.

Animals flank her sides, but Mary
has never seen sheep or the restless
breath of cows until this cold morning.

She clasps her hands together. Her fingers
steeple toward stars, but her eyes,
speckled with fires of light, point down.

Her clothes are a casing, a chrysalis;
the stable walls drape around her. Something
bangs on the boards, a blacksmith's

hammer, the heavy
thump of a leaden heart.

Supermarket in Autumn

Rains enter the supermarket,
the relief of rain washing
        the epidermal layer
of insects off foods, off
rows of cans, pink
and green in their skins.

Muted monologues,
supermarket checkers, heads
bowed over scanners, they grab
        the frozen meat,
its resin-baked bones.
Nodding, blowing, rows and rows

of ripening corn reach out.
The stands of cornsilk wave,
        wave in the cornstalk wind.
Rise and fall of land, etched,
crisscrossed with crops, soaked
with rain, dried, soaked again.

The women are weeders, gatherers,
their hands bend and pull.
        Children, asleep in carts,
mouth words to break the dark.
So much is seasonal, so much
        drift; fish float belly up.

Loons hoot over the lake, rocks
        split the sound.

Devil's Potato Patch

Changing weather,
the blankets
on the bed—always
too hot, too cold,
take them off, put them on,
passage of tick, tock,
the clock, bald, jutting up
from the ice flows,
kettles, and rocks.

Erratics settle
on a ground so inclined
only Sisyphus
could restrain them.
The brook raves
below the road,
and the fine-edged
instruments of leaves
creak in the keening wind.

No one lives here
anymore—just rocks
upended. Ancestors boil
out of the parched hill,
our imaginary home,
Sisyphus—this is
the myth that drives us.

Bottomland

Evening tidings, the preparations,
each nestle, each cheep, like chicks calling,
the winnowing anomie, all
come to call too late, come
to call for sleep.

How a mother can change from angel
to sour mudqueen of all decay
by those who feel the sting, by those
who cry out.

Flail my heart upon the stone
in the grove near the riverbank,
rushing water to the river break.
Even the known becomes unknowable.
Their small eyes look at me like chicks
gathered against rain, staved.

Thin rivulets of fear, running-away-
with-itself fear, fearful fear.
No one can talk to you, no one
can listen, no one can touch you.
This is not stillness, this is not the keeper
of the estuary of the deep.

Don't forget me, don't forget
that hill the horses cantered
you down to the bottomland.
From this stone, ageless heart,
remember your mother,
a mother who loved her children.

Notes

The poems "Cracked Piano," "Plank Walk," and "No Occurrence of an Exciting Nature" were derived from letters written by my great-grandfather, Peter Rawson Taft, when he resided at the Cincinnati Sanitarium, Private Hospital for the Insane, to his father, Alphonso Taft.

The poems "Something Wrong," "Causes of Mortification," and "Common Cases of Insanity" were derived from letters written by W. S. Chipley, M.D., Superintendent, Cincinnati Sanitarium, Private Hospital for the Insane, about Peter R. Taft to Mrs. Peter R. Taft and to his father, Alphonso Taft.

Regarding "The Lunatic Ball," in the latter half of the nineteenth century, superintendents at insane asylums often held balls considered therapeutic for their patients. Spectators were sometimes invited.

The epigraph for "Quiet, with Trees" is from "The Birdsong," published in *The Collected Poems of William Carlos Williams*, Volume II (2001), p. 128.

Acknowledgments

Grateful acknowledgment is made to the following publications in which these poems first appeared, sometimes in different versions:

A Poetry Congeries, Connotation Press: An Online Artifact: "Valentine"
A Slant of Light: Contemporary Women Writers of the Hudson Valley,
 edited by Laurance Carr and Jan Zlotnik Schmidt, Codhill Press,
 2013: "Wind Innuendo"
Bared: Contemporary Poetry and Art on Bras and Breasts, edited by
 Laura Madeline Wiseman, Les Femmes Folles Books, 2017:
 "Nothing's Holding Up Nothing"
Big City Lit: "Missing Link"
Blackbird: "Idiot's Guide to Counting," "Surfaces," "Supermarket in
 Autumn"
Bottomland: A Novel by Michelle Hoover, Grove/Atlantic, 2016: epigraph
 from Stever poem "Bottomland"
cahoodaloodaling: "The Lunatic Ball," "Causes of Mortification,"
 "Something Wrong"
Cincinnati Review: "Why So Many Poets Come from Ohio," "The True
 Story of Eugene"
Collateral Damage: A Pirene's Fountain Anthology, edited by Ami Kaye,
 Glass Lyre Press, 2018: "Nothing's Holding Up Nothing"
Connecticut Review: "Splitting Wood," "Raven's Rock," "Queen City"
Elsewhere: "The Hudson Line" first published as "Offerings"
en(compass), The Poetry Caravan Anthology, edited by Usha Akella,
 Yuganta Press, 2001: "Splitting Wood," "Invisible Fence" (first
 published as "Suburban Sightings")
enskyment Online Anthology of Poetry, edited by Dan Masterson,
 enskyment.org, 2018: "Idiot's Guide to Counting," "Splitting Wood,"
 "My Mother Is Dying"

G.W. Review: "Quiet, with Trees," first published as "An Ample Silence"

Hanging Loose and *The Harvard Advocate:* "I have been my arm"

Heron Tree: "Plank Walk"

Joys of the Table: An Anthology of Culinary Verse, edited by Sally Zakariya, Richer Resources Publications, 2015: "Drought"

Nasty Women Poets: An Unapologetic Anthology of Subversive Verse, edited by Grace Bauer and Julie Kane, Lost Horse Press, 2017: "Horse Fair"

No More Masks (first edition), edited by Florence Howe and Ellen Bass, Doubleday & Co., 1973: "I have been my arm"

Phoebe: "Hand"

Poem-A-Day Series, poets.org, The Academy of American Poets (March 23, 2016): "For Sale"

Poet Lore: "Nothing's Holding Up Nothing"

Poetry Flash: "My Mother Is Dying," "Strange Familiarities of Death"

Poetry.Magazine.com, edited by Andrena Zawinski, Fall, 2014: "Splitting Wood"

Poetry South: "The Cracked Piano," "The Worst Mother," "Stepmother," "Animal Crackers"

Prairie Schooner: "Bottomland" (first published as "Bottom Land")

Rattapallax: "Wind Innuendo"

Reflecting Pool: Poets and the Creative Process, edited by Laurance Carr, Codhill Press, 2018: "Idiot's Guide to Counting," "My Mother Is Dying"

Salamander: "Van Gogh to His Mistress"

Sarah Lawrence Review: "Beulah Reid," "Devil's Potato Patch"

The Original Van Gogh's Ear Anthology, theoriginalvangoghsearanthology. com: "Van Gogh to His Mistress"

The Same: "Horse Fair" (first published as "Seer and Seen"), "Cult of the Virgin"

Sow's Ear Poetry Review: "Yellow Raincoat," "Invisible Fence" (first published as "Suburban Sightings")

Valley Voices: "Glimpse of an Infant Eating"

Veils, Halos, and Shackles: International Poetry on the Oppression and Empowerment of Women, edited by Charles Fishman and Smita Sahay, Kasva Press, 2016: "Nothing's Holding Up Nothing"

Women Write Resistance: Poets Resist Gender Violence, edited by Laura Madeline Wiseman, Hyacinth Girl Press, 2013: "Splitting Wood"

Some poems were reprinted in the chapbooks *The Hudson Line* (Main Street Rag, 2012) and *The Lunatic Ball* (Kattywompus Press, 2015).

Special thanks to my Slapering Hol Press co-editors, Peggy Ellsberg and Jennifer Franklin, for their inspiration. I would also like to thank other members of my writing workshop—Sally Bliumis-Dunn, Marion S. Brown, and Joan Falk—for their insight and support. Also, Thanks to Jesse Wright for his introduction. Thanks to Richard Foerster, David Kutz-Marks, and Julie Danho for their invaluable input on editing and copyediting. I would like to thank CavanKerry Editor Baron Wormser for his thoughtful edits and commentary and Starr Troup for her consideration and advice. Finally, I give thanks to my husband, Donald W. Stever, for his brilliance and vision, and to my children, Dave, Jamie, and Heather, and to Johnnie Alexander.

CavanKerry's Mission

CavanKerry Press is committed to expanding the reach of poetry to a general readership by publishing poets whose works explore the emotional and psychological landscapes of everyday life.

Other Books in the LaurelBooks Series

Cracked Piano has been set in DIN OT, a realist sans-serif typeface based on DIN-Mittelschrift and DIN-Engschrift, as defined in the German standard DIN 1451. DIN is an acronym for Deutsches Institut für Normung (German Institute of Standardization).